The Space Between

Poetry for Reflection

Pam Noble

Write Angles Press

The Space Between

Copyright © Pam Noble 2025

pam@pamnoble.com.au

The right of Pam Noble to be identified as the author of this work has been asserted by her in accordance with the Copyright Amendment (Moral Rights) Act 2000.

This work is copyright. Apart from any use as permitted under the Copyright Act 1968, no part of this publication may be reproduced, stored in a retrieval system or transmitted in any form by any means electronic, mechanical, photocopying, recording or otherwise without the prior written consent of the author or publisher.

First published in 2025 by WRITE ANGLES PRESS (JUST RIGHT WORDS)

www.justrightwords.com.au

ISBN: (print) 978-1-7642378-3-3

Cover design: Triandhika Anjani

 A catalogue record for this book is available from the National Library of Australia

Dedication

The poems in this book were written as a result of the
shared human experience of suffering, which I encounter
in my work as a counsellor.
Through my poetry, I hope to enable a shared connection
and a feeling that we are not alone.

Contents

The Space Between	1
Introduction	2
FIRST COMES STILLNESS	5
Possibility	7
If only	8
The tree	10
Reflect (i)	13
AND IN THAT STILLNESS ...	23
Shrinking	25
Essence	26

Words	28
Reflect (ii)	29
LET GO	37
Shame	39
The critic	40
I can't	41
Reflect (iii)	43
OPEN UP, MAKE ROOM	51
This moment	53
Motivation	54
One thought	56
Not quite	58
The box	60
One day when	62
Reflect (iv)	63
ALLOW	71
Lessons	73
I just want to say	74
Alone	76

Loss	78
Clean	80
Reflect (v)	83
BE PRESENT	91
It's raining inside	93
Restless	94
Waiting	96
Humming	98
Reflect (vi)	101
AND ...	107
One plate	109
Aged	110
Now	111
And	112
Faces in the moon	114
Just because	116
Some people	118
What if	120
Love	122

Aloneness	124
Tea	125
Reflect (vii)	127
About the author	131

The Space Between

In order to smell the roses ... you need to notice them first.

Introduction

This poetry collection is a result of my passion for personal growth and development. As a counsellor, on a daily basis I experience clients who are stuck. The reasons are as varied as the clouds moving across the sky. The experiences range from traumatic to varying degrees of anxiety, stress, grief, depression or situations perhaps arising from conflicts within a relationship. By the time they find the courage to seek support, my clients have developed a mind and body that no longer serves them to live a full and meaningful life. They are drifting in an ocean of fear, anxiety, anger or self-doubt; or they are frozen, staring at their lives with no motivation to move.

In today's fast-paced society, driven by technology and the ongoing pursuit of personal and collective goals, the simple skill of stillness, space and reflection are rarely, if ever, experienced. Without space we are unable to notice our behaviours, our feelings and our emotions. In turn, this minimises our power to make wise choices – choices that align with our values and beliefs, and that are helpful to build our own self efficacy.

Poetry is a personal thing, with each individual taking what they need from the words. Some of the poems in this collection have been published in poetry magazines or journals, and some are new. Some will resonate with you, and some won't. Take what you need from them. Allow them to prompt and guide you to reflect, finding that space that comes with stillness, with slowing down, with breathing in the moment and with a sense of being enough. Pages are inserted at the end of each section for you to do your own inner work.

I hope you use this book as your own. Write in it. Scribble down thoughts as you go. Highlight, cross out, and reflect in whatever way works for you. If it is not for you at this moment, put it back on the shelf until you are ready. If reading the poems alone is enough, then just do that. There are no rules.

Many of my poems asked to be heard. During my time of stillness, some poems worked their way into my consciousness. They came for their own purposes and would not be silenced.

I invite you to use your stillness to find your voice and your medium of expressing the thoughts that also want to be heard.

Pam

FIRST COMES STILLNESS

Possibility

If I could sit with experience,

feel the not knowing as knowing,

lean into possibility

open, curious, aware.

If I could ...

If only

If only

I could be with myself,
sit with myself.

If only

I could awaken myself,
walk with myself.

If only

I could sustain myself
care for myself
unravel myself
be true to myself.

If only

I could find the
essence of myself.

If only ...

The tree

In the chaos of the day
the emails, messages,
work schedules, meetings,
sometimes you see a window,
outside that window
is a tree, its branches
strong, sturdy outstretched
from its trunk, embedded
into the ground, where leaves,
yellow, red, gold, scatter,
make a playground,
for the children, laughing

tossing them above their heads.

Sometimes we can close our eyes

and we can see.

Reflect (i)

What are you noticing as you read the poems?

After reading the poems, what has come up for you?

Is there some part of you that is not being heard?

Not understood?

Is there some part of you that would like to change?

AND IN THAT STILLNESS ...

Shrinking

I am shrinking
drawing into myself
slowly slipping
inward, dragging the curtains
shutting out the hum of
iPad, iPhone, computer,
the ping of
emails, messages,
the shrill of the phone,
shrinking
dripping, drop by drop
back into me.

Essence

Embodied in the silence of the mind

a purple haze

opens up

expands

present in the wholeness

welded to the earth

yet floating

no words

no voice

drifting ...

a fly buzzes circling round and back

a soft breeze, gentle

THE SPACE BETWEEN

feathered

the smell of jasmine

sweet, strong

honey smooth

soliciting childhood

safe secure

entering then leaving

refuge from a broken self.

Words

Words float across the
landscape of my mind,
fragments of meaning
scatter like autumn leaves
fuelled by the afternoon breeze,
a puzzle, I try to find the
whole picture, to make sense
of something that there is
no sense to make,
there is no story
just words.

Reflect (ii)

What words, images or moments arose from the poems?

Can you describe those moments?

What did you see as you read the poems?

LET GO

Shame

The voice in my head
scratches like a trapped bird,
squeaking, trying to be heard,
to rise above the cacophony
of voices, demanding
echoing through the day.
The night bird, defeated with the effort
folds its wings and turns into itself
holding tight to shame.

The critic

Words stick like superglue to my skin,
I can't erase the memory of them,
ammunition, a direct hit,
shrapnel shattering my
weeping soul, regurgitating
wounds, depleting
the rainbow of
my dreams.

I can't

I can't sit outside in the sun today
and feed the birds with my crumbs.
I can't watch bees buzz around my petunias
or dig the gorse in between.
I can't potter around my study
looking for books to read.
But
I can open the door today if the wind
whispers to you, my plea.

Reflect (iii)

Did anything move within as you read these poems?

Did any feelings arise? Can you put a name to them?

If not a name, can you draw an image of your feelings?

OPEN UP, MAKE ROOM

This moment

Open up

right now

be curious,

imprints

in the heart

in the soul,

live on

in our memories.

If we are lost

unaware

our canvas is blank.

Motivation

I sit waiting

for something,

I wonder

if waiting

or sitting

is a way

and if

I sit and wonder

as I wait,

is sitting

and waiting

THE SPACE BETWEEN

in fact

something?

One thought

If I had but one thought
it would be
"I am kind."
If that one thought gave voice
I would ask
"Are you kind?"
If that person had one thought
"Am I kind?"
If they could ask just one person
and that one person could
ask one person
until each person

asked

"Am I kind?"

Maybe being kind

would make all the difference.

Not quite

I live in limbo, not quite
forfeiting perfection
fulfillment, forgoing
a future foreseen
for essentially
amnesia.
I live on the outside
infused with anomalies
creating illusions
a reality of normality
in essence
just flawed.

THE SPACE BETWEEN

I live in a time zone

uniquely obscure

frozen in focus

developing solutions

to problems

unsolved.

I live in loneliness, not alone

waiting

wondering

watching

almost becoming but

not quite.

The box

I am delicate,
plain, unvarnished,
lined with soft pink cotton,
cushioned with fine fibre
to hold the secrets in.
I am well worn,
used frequently,
testimony to past generations,
lid closed tight,
secured with lock and key.
I am kept hidden
away from prying eyes,

coveted, yet feared,

taken from place to place,

mandated, controlled.

I dream, imagine a

future untethered,

free to abandon

the fear and pain,

wounds, open, bleeding,

vulnerable, seen.

One day when

One stormy day

when

sugar falls from the sky

half fills my cup

I will feel the

sweetness of life

one day

when ...

Reflect (iv)

What did these poems suggest to you?

Is there a need within you that wants to be heard?

Is there room to allow that need to be heard? If so, how?

ALLOW

Lessons

I'm a slow learner
taking the lessons of life
turning them inward, analysing,
interpreting the data
the same pattern emerges.
Unfolded, a perfect shape
a criss-cross of
contradictions, contrary
to the evidence yet
still, I do not learn,
and I begin the lesson
yet again.

I just want to say

I just want to say,
there are some things
sometimes
in some places
where some things
just don't seem right.

I just want to say
there are some people
sometimes
in some places
where some people

THE SPACE BETWEEN

say things that hurt.

I just want to say

there are some times

in some places

where some things

and some people

make me want to weep ...

Alone

I sit, listen to the birdsong,

warm air caressing my face,

soft whisper of leaves,

fresh scent of eucalypt,

this moment is enough.

"What are you doing today?"
"Where are you going?"
"Why are you here?"

Questions vibrating the

space I chose.

THE SPACE BETWEEN

A space to be
free from my own voice.
I am not lonely.
Why is it that I can not
be free to be alone?

Loss

I close my eyes and wait for the memory
somewhere it is hidden
amongst blood and sinew,
I want it to spill out,
yet it is trapped there
like a caged bird,
pecking at the bars.
I feel you in the beat of my heart,
my pulse, rapid, erratic,
I know we were walking,
there was sleet, cold
ice dripping, like now

THE SPACE BETWEEN

my eyes flowing with tears

   I wait for the memory

      but nothing comes.

Clean

I just want to clean.
Scrub away bitter memories,
rub and polish until a new spirit
shines through.
I want to fill a bucket
with hope and new dreams
throw over the flames of my past
and renew.
I want to live
awakened to the purity
of a new beginning,

open, aware,

filled with awe!

Reflect (v)

In thinking about the poems, leading up to and including the last section, what have you noticed?

In thinking about where you are right now, are you being who you truly want to be?

Is there something in the words, images or blank spaces that reflect back to you? If so, what?

BE PRESENT

It's raining inside

It's raining inside
the damp, bleak wantonness,
hollow, emptiness,
slow, same, darkness,
seeping into
the heart,
grey, cloudy,
cold.
It's raining inside,
outside the sun
shines bright.

Restless

I am in this world,

this grass, barren, crisp,

this wind ferocious, wild,

this angry sky swirling with dark clouds

waiting to burst.

I am in this place,

this seat, well worn,

leather cracked, torn,

desk-cluttered pages, scattered, neglected,

screaming attention.

THE SPACE BETWEEN

I am in this body,

this breath shallow,

these muscles tense,

this mind wandering, restless,

wanting to come home

to myself.

Waiting

I've been waiting for rain,
sweet smell of fresh
damp earth, air crisp,
the rhythmic patter on
our old tin roof.

I've been waiting for
dust to settle, dry
cracked paddocks, scorched
by relentless heat,
sheep just wool and bones.

THE SPACE BETWEEN

I've been waiting for hope
to splash down, dance
over boulders, fill the creeks
breathe life back into
the belly of the land ...

I've been waiting
but it has not come.

Humming

I am sitting with my wounded soul
crossed legged on the wooden floor
in a dark room with strangers,
on close inspection eight,
sitting on soft yoga mats,
their hands folded in laps,
smooth browed, eyes focused
and then humming, startled
I sweep the room wondering,
low, slow, not like a bee, not a bird,
a sound foreign, breathtaking
it rises, I feel my throat open,

THE SPACE BETWEEN

my eyes close, I am there in the room
humming, humming, humming,
my body is filled with it,
lungs expand with it,
heart welcomes it,
humming, humming, humming.

Reflect (vi)

After reading this section of poems and reflecting on the title of this collection, what does it mean to you to be present?

Right here, right now, reflect. Let go. Write.

AND ...

One plate

One plate
stares back at me
from the soap suds.
One plate
will be there tomorrow
and the next day.
Next to the one fork
swirling in the bubbles
alone.

Aged

Thoughts untethered I sit beside the fire
wondering, a life lived, or life not so.
Beside me on a mat, a dog, breathing
slow, steady, music to lonely ears.
Outside grass and weeds unite now untamed,
flowers, fight for light, live and die, unseen.
Late afternoon sun filters through net curtains,
dust moats float and settle on the table nearby.
The mantle clock ticks in rhythm to my sighs
eyes unblinking, I look towards the doorway,
waiting, remembering
as time drifts by.

Now

Cobwebs trail across the

painted tin.

A dead spider hangs from its invisible thread,

across the floor

a lizard slithers,

hurriedly changing

directions, over the mat

around the old boot,

out into the fresh cool air.

And

She sits with her laptop and her latte,
legs crossed, cushioned in the folds
of the big leather chair,
sipping, typing.

Her hair askew from the loose band
flops across her eyes, head bent,
fingers nimble,
typing, sipping,
other people gather in the doorway,
chatting, laughing, gesturing
with their hands.

THE SPACE BETWEEN

I sit, my well-worn runners push into the floor,

hands shaky, pouring tea from the pot

into a cup, whilst

watching.

Faces in the moon

I see faces in the moon

looking down, tears dripping

from the sky as the stars

emerge from the shadow of the clouds,

magic happens ...

Fear dissipates into the darkness.

I stand barefoot on the damp earth

let the rain wash away

my pain,

THE SPACE BETWEEN

nocturnal sounds permeate the silence

I am not alone.

Soaked clothes envelop my skin,

arms outstretched I howl,

a primordial urge to let go …

Just because

I see it in your eyes
the sideways glance,
just because
I ride the wave of your sigh
feel the space like a void
you move on.
You don't see
the thunderous roar of
my heart pumping
the needle point pain
of sensations crippling
my body.

THE SPACE BETWEEN

Just because

you don't hear

the words fighting

danger, danger,

pushing the scream from

my throat,

propelling my legs.

Just because

I run,

I scream,

you all turn

fear dripping from your skin.

Just because

you don't see me.

Some people

Some people

screw up,

make mistakes,

move on,

remake bigger mistakes,

behave badly,

treat people poorly,

set their own agenda,

control others' agendas,

manipulate a path

towards achievement,

aggrandising

righteousness of

their opinions,

whilst

some people

just hang on ...

What if

What if you saw me

understood,

accepted

my rawness,

my weakness,

and my fears.

Would you define me?

Would you then give me

a label,

a story,

then meet me

again, see me

eyes wide open.

What then would you see?

What if you unknew

what you knew

and renewed

our meeting,

my newness,

then forever new.

What if ...

Love

I grip the cloth, hands clenched
back and forth,
heart pumping, arms stiff,
wiping dust from the
woodfire heater,
tiny shards of bark
splinters of hand-cut sticks,
scrubbing
footprints from my husband's boot,
crumbs
from my grandson's toast,
fine white hairs

from our Cavalier

following me as I go,

my hands loosen,

the cloth goes limp,

I open my heart

to love.

Aloneness

I am sorry

my aloneness scares you.

Feel free

to live your life,

as I am living

mine alone.

Tea

Love emanates from the teapot
covered with a pink and white cosy,
crocheted, stitch by stitch
with hands that were made to give.

Reflect (vii)

Is this your chance? Your blank canvas?

About the author

Pam Noble is a counsellor, coach and avid reader. A family person, her daughters and son are her best friends. Pam also loves spending time with her grandchildren, and especially enjoys watching them with their sports and dancing. When the weather permits, she loves to go fishing. Sometimes, even when the seas are rough, Pam can be found with her husband and son, trawling for tuna at their favourite fishing spot, Eagle Hawk Neck on the east coast of Tasmania.

www.ingramcontent.com/pod-product-compliance
Lightning Source LLC
Chambersburg PA
CBHW030232100526
44583CB00013BA/897